WIND, SOLAR, AND GEOTHERMAL
POWER
FROM CONCEPT TO CONSUMER

BY STEVEN OTFINOSKI

CHILDREN'S PRESS®

An Imprint of Scholastic Inc.

CONTENT CONSULTANT
Ken Fedor

PHOTOGRAPHS ©: Photos ©: cover: Dennis Schroeder/NREL 27196/National Renewable Energy Laboratory; 3: Lowell Georgia/Science Source; 4 left: The Granger Collection; 4 right: Russ Curtis/Science Source; 5 left: Ingram Publishing/Newscom; 5 right: Washington Imaging/Alamy Images; 6: AP Images; 8: BeBa/Iberfoto/The Image Works; 9: The Granger Collection; 10: North Wind Picture Archives; 11 top: Steve Hamblin/Alamy Images; 11 bottom: The Granger Collection; 12: Apic/Getty Images; 13: Mark Williamson/Science Source; 14 top: Roger Viollet Collection/Getty Images; 14 bottom: The Granger Collection; 15 top: Jenoche/Shutterstock, Inc.; 15 bottom: Jim West/age fotostock/Superstock, Inc.; 16: Martin Rietze/Westend61/Superstock, Inc.; 17: Steve Hamblin/Alamy Images; 18: Topher Donahue/Media Bakery; 20: Tsuneo Yamashita/Media Bakery; 21: Ivern Photo/Media Bakery; 22 top: Bob Daemmrich/Alamy Images; 22 bottom: Jeff McIntosh/The Canadian Press/AP Images; 23 top: Rex Features via AP Images; 23 bottom: Christoph Schmidt/picture-alliance/dpa/AP Images; 24: Russ Curtis/Science Source; 25: Lowell Georgia/Science Source; 26 left: Jim West/Media Bakery; 26 right: CreativeNature R.Zwerver/Shutterstock, Inc.; 27 left: CreativeNature R.Zwerver/Shutterstock, Inc.; 27 right: Stephen Lock/i-Images/Polaris/Newscom; 28: Brennan Linsley/AP Images; 29: Mark Boulton/Alamy Images; 30: Patrick Pleul/picture-alliance/dpa/AP Images; 32: Lisa-Blue/iStockphoto; 33: Theodore Clutter/Science Source; 36: Martin Barraud/Media Bakery; 37: Ingram Publishing/Newscom; 38: lever mikaël/Alamy Images; 39: Daniel Reinhardt/picturealliance/dpa/AP Images; 40 left: Nic Hamilton Photographic/Alamy Images; 40 right, 41: Scott Barbour/Getty Images; 42: Media Bakery; 43: Joe Raedle/Getty Images; 44: Robert Nickelsberg/Getty Images; 46: Seb Oliver/Cultura Limited/Superstock, Inc.; 47: Simon Battensby/Media Bakery; 48: U.S. Department of Energy; 49 top: Jim West/Alamy Images; 49 bottom: Dennis Schroeder/NREL 31128/National Renewable Energy Laboratory; 50: Sunpix Travel/Alamy Images; 51: AOC Photo/Alamy Images; 52: Washington Imaging/Alamy Images; 53: Aurora Photos/Alamy Images; 54 left: Michele and Tom Grimm/Alamy Images; 54 right: Gary Crabbe/age fotostock/Superstock, Inc.; 55 top: Jim Holmes/Media Bakery; 55 bottom: Gary Crabbe/age fotostock/Superstock, Inc.; 56: Julie Jacobson/AP Images; 57: Solar Design Associates, Inc; 58: Dennis Schroeder/NREL 29513/National Renewable Energy Laboratory; 59: © 2012 atelierdna.com.

LIBRARY OF CONGRESS CATALOGING-IN-PUBLICATION DATA
Otfinoski, Steven, author.
 Wind, solar, and geothermal power : from concept to consumer / by Steven Otfinoski.
    pages cm. — (Calling all innovators : a career for you)
 Summary: "Learn about the history of alternative energy and find out what it takes to make it in this exciting career field." — Provided by publisher.
 Includes bibliographical references and index.
 ISBN 978-0-531-21897-6 (library binding : alk. paper) — ISBN 978-0-531-21915-7 (pbk. : alk. paper)
 1. Renewable energy sources — Juvenile literature. 2. Renewable natural resources — Juvenile literature.
 3. Energy industries — Vocational guidance — Juvenile literature. I. Title.
  TJ808.2.084 2016
  333.79'4 — dc23   2014049200

All rights reserved. Published in 2016 by Children's Press, an imprint of Scholastic Inc.
Printed in the United States of America 113

1 2 3 4 5 6 7 8 9 10 R 25 24 23 22 21 20 19 18 17 16

CALLING ALL INNOVATORS
A CAREER FOR YOU

Science, technology, engineering, arts, and math are the fields that drive innovation. Whether they are finding ways to make our lives easier or developing the latest entertainment, the people who work in these fields are changing the world for the better. Do you have what it takes to join the ranks of today's greatest innovators? Read on to discover if a career in the exciting world of wind, solar, and geothermal power is for you.

TABLE *of* CONTENTS

According to legend, the ancient Greeks used mirrors to attack enemies with solar energy.

Wind farms are a common sight in many parts of the world today.

A number of skilled experts are involved in any solar power installation project.

Workers face unique challenges when bringing solar power to older buildings.

Many gas stations ran out of fuel completely during the 1973 energy crisis.

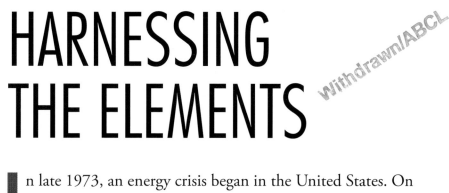

HARNESSING THE ELEMENTS

I n late 1973, an energy crisis began in the United States. On October 17, the oil-rich Arab nations halted oil shipments to the United States in retaliation for U.S. support of Israel in a war against Egypt and Syria.

Overnight, the price of oil rose from $3 per barrel to $12. Gasoline, which is made from oil, was suddenly in short supply.

Arab nations resumed selling oil to the United States in March 1974, but Americans felt the effects of the energy crisis for the rest of the decade. For the first time, many people realized they could not always depend on fossil fuels such as oil, coal, and natural gas. They began to consider **renewable** sources of energy, such as wind, solar, and geothermal power. For many Americans, these alternative energy sources were fresh ideas. However, people had actually been using them since the dawn of history.

SOLAR ENERGY LANDMARKS

1839	1954	1968	1979
Alexandre-Edmond Becquerel discovers a process for converting light energy to electricity.	Scientists at Bell Telephone Laboratories use silicon to build a more efficient solar cell.	The first wearable solar-powered device, a wristwatch, goes on sale.	Under President Jimmy Carter, 32 solar panels are installed on the roof of the White House.

FREE AS THE WIND

Wind, sun, and the earth are three natural sources of seemingly inexhaustible power. While fossil fuels such as coal and oil will eventually run out, renewable sources of energy will be with us for millions of years.

Believe it or not, wind is created by the sun. As sunlight warms the air unevenly, hot air rises and cool air rushes in to take its place. This produces wind. The ancient Egyptians were the first people to harness the power of the wind for their own uses. Beginning around 3200 BCE, they used it to propel sailboats on the Nile River.

During the 10th century, Persians put wind to work on land with the creation of the windmill. Early mills used wind power to grind grain so it could be made into bread. These mills looked nothing like the more modern windmills. They rotated horizontally and had cloth sails instead of blades.

The first vertical windmills, which look much like the ones used today, were built in Rome. By about 1100, the technology had spread to Europe. Windmills became especially popular in the Netherlands, where they were used to pump water out of lakes and marshes.

Ancient Egyptian sailboats were the first machines built to rely on wind power.

LARGE CLOTH SAIL FOR CATCHING WIND

Inventor Charles F. Brush was a pioneer of wind energy technology.

MILLS AND TURBINES

Eventually, people started using windmills to power **generators** and produce electricity. This practice was most popular in rural communities without access to wiring and cables. American inventor Charles F. Brush created the first **turbines** in 1888. These were large windmills capable of providing electricity for several homes at a time. Over the years, people built larger and more effective turbines. In 1941, engineers built a massive windmill on a hilltop in Vermont called Grandpa's Knob. Its 75-foot (23 meter) blades made it around 10 times larger than any other windmill in the world at the time. It supplied electricity throughout the surrounding area. However, advances in wind power came to a halt as fossil fuels became popular in the 1950s. Many wind turbines fell into disuse until interest in alternative energy began to increase as a result of the energy crisis in the 1970s.

PAST MARVELS

BLADE SHAPE DESIGNED TO CATCH WIND

Wooden-bladed windmills looked much different from the sleek turbines of modern wind farms.

FROM WOOD TO STEEL

Wooden blades were the norm for windmills until about 1870. By that time, manufacturers were able to cheaply produce steel in large quantities. Steel was lighter, more durable, and able to catch wind more efficiently than wood. As a result, steel blades soon replaced most wooden blades, greatly increasing the productivity of windmills. They were particularly effective in small windmills. In fact, they worked so well that new parts were added to many steel-bladed mills to slow them down and allow the water pumps inside to work at a normal speed.

Many steel-bladed windmills still stand on rural farms today.

WINDMILLS ON THE GREAT PLAINS

Steel-bladed windmills were a blessing for the people who began to settle the Great Plains of the American West in the years following the Civil War. Little rain fell on the plains in summer, and there were few nearby bodies of water. Windmills allowed the settlers to pump water from wells deep underground. The water was then collected in storage tanks for use throughout the year.

Some windmills pumped water for the steam-powered railroad trains that provided transportation across the vast plains. Others powered farm machines such as corn shellers and feed grinders. By the 1930s, some farmers were using windmills to generate electricity for their homes.

It is estimated that more than six million small windmills were in use across America between 1850 and 1970. They became a common sight on the flat western landscape. Many older people who grew up on the Great Plains look back on their old windmills with affection. These remarkable devices brought life and prosperity to communities and families who couldn't have survived without them. ✳

A windmill was often a necessary part of making a new home in the Great Plains.

Alexandre-Edmond Becquerel's innovations kicked off the era of using solar power to generate electricity.

POWER FROM THE SUN

There is no greater energy source in our solar system than the sun. This enormous star gives off huge amounts of bright light and reaches surface temperatures of around 10,000 degrees Fahrenheit (5,538 degrees Celsius). Each hour, the sun generates enough energy to meet Earth's total needs for a year.

Ancient peoples harnessed the power of the sun by building their homes to face it and receive its warm rays. The Greeks were pioneers in taking advantage of solar energy. They used the sun's light to start fires to boil water and create steam power.

In 1839, French physicist Alexandre-Edmond Becquerel discovered a scientific process for converting sunlight into electricity. This enabled later innovators to create the first **photovoltaic cells**.

FROM CELLS TO PANELS

Photovoltaic cells remained little more than a curiosity for more than a century. Early versions could convert only about 1 percent of the sun's light into electricity. In 1954, scientists at Bell Telephone Laboratories used a material called silicon to build a more efficient photovoltaic cell. It was six times more effective than earlier cells at generating electricity.

A few years later, *Vanguard I* became the first **satellite** to be powered by solar cells. It absorbed sunlight and stored its energy in batteries. This way it still had power while traveling in Earth's shadow, out of the sunlight.

As with wind power, interest in solar power increased during the 1970s energy crisis. Solar cells were redesigned to make them more efficient and less expensive to produce. Groups of cells were joined together to form solar panels, which could generate enough electricity to provide power for an entire building. By the 1980s, engineers had figured out how to build huge solar power plants capable of producing even larger amounts of electricity.

SOLAR PANELS

Vanguard I *was equipped with six solar panels.*

Archimedes is most famous for his contributions to the field of mathematics.

MORE THAN JUST A CLOSER LOOK

Though photovoltaic cells were not invented until the 19th century, humans had already been using other materials to harness solar energy for hundreds of years. For example, the ancient Greeks understood that mirrors could be used to direct sunlight and concentrate its strength.

Instead of glass, the earliest mirrors were made from pieces of polished metal that reflected light. They were first used in about 3500 BCE. The Greeks improved mirror-making techniques in around 320 BCE and even established a school for mirror makers.

ARCHIMEDES'S MIRROR

According to legend, the Greek scientist Archimedes used mirrors and solar energy to help to win a battle against the ancient Romans. When Roman ships attacked Archimedes's home city of Syracuse in 212 BCE, the great thinker used giant mirrors to target sunlight at them. The ships caught fire due to the concentrated sun rays. They were reduced to ashes from about 500 feet (152 m) away.

Archimedes directs Greek soldiers in aiming concentrated solar beams at Roman ships.

A SOLAR TOWER

In 1982, the U.S. Department of Energy (DOE) built a solar "power tower" in the Mojave Desert near Barstow, California. Called Solar One, the tower was topped with a device that collected reflected light from thousands of tiny sun-tracking mirrors called heliostats. The light's heat is used to turn circulating water into steam. The steam powers a generator that produces electricity.

Power towers can capture a great deal of energy, but they also take up a lot of space.

SOLAR ENERGY ENTERS THROUGH GLASS

HEAT FROM SOLAR ENERGY IS TRAPPED INSIDE GREENHOUSE

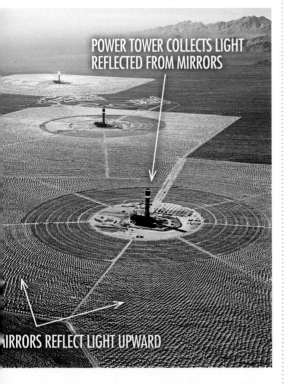

POWER TOWER COLLECTS LIGHT REFLECTED FROM MIRRORS

MIRRORS REFLECT LIGHT UPWARD

Greenhouses allow gardeners to grow fruits, flowers, and other plants in a variety of climates.

THE GREENHOUSE EFFECT

Like mirrors, glass that is plain and transparent can magnify the sun's energy. Greenhouses have been used for thousands of years to grow plants when it is too cold for them to thrive outdoors. The slanted, glass-paneled roof of a greenhouse allows huge amounts of sunlight to enter the building. The sunlight's heat is trapped in the greenhouse, keeping the interior warm even when the air outside is chilly. ☀

POWER FROM INSIDE THE EARTH

Like the sun, Earth itself produces heat energy. The term *geothermal* comes from the Greek words "geo" and "thermo." Combined, these words mean "heated by the earth." The heat of Earth's inner core melts rock in the mantle, which is the layer between the outer crust and the central core. As the rock melts, it becomes a molten material called magma. The hot magma seeps upward through breaks in Earth's crust. Its heat causes underground water sources to heat up and generate steam. The steam then rises to the surface to create geysers and hot springs such as those found at Yellowstone National Park.

People eventually realized that they could make use of the hot water and steam that came from the ground. Thousands of years ago, Native Americans bathed in hot springs and used the heated water to cook food and clean clothes. Around 100 CE, the Romans heated their homes by running water from hot springs through pipes under buildings.

Yellowstone National Park's Castle Geyser is named for its castle-like shape.

STEAM AND WATER
ERUPT DUE TO
GEOTHERMAL ENERGY

Northern California is home to many geothermal power plants.

FROM STEAM TO ELECTRICITY

In 1904, the Italian scientist Piero Ginori Conti discovered that steam rising up from underground could be used to generate electricity. This discovery led him to build the world's first geothermal power plant in Tuscany, Italy.

The first geothermal power plant in the United States was constructed in 1921 in Northern California. It was not able to produce much energy, and it was soon closed. However, scientists and engineers continued to improve geothermal technology. In 1960, a new geothermal power plant near the same site began supplying electricity to the region. A much bigger success than the effort in 1921, the new plant operated for more than 30 years. Today, there are more than 60 geothermal power plants operating in the United States.

In 2009, geothermal power accounted for less than 1 percent of the world's energy. However, scientists predict that this power from the earth may fulfill as much as 20 percent of our energy needs by 2050.

Many modern houses are built from the ground up to rely on solar power.

CHAPTER TWO

RENEWABLE ENERGY SOURCES TODAY

You wake up as the alarm clock next to your bed begins ringing. It's cold outside, but it's nice and warm in your bedroom thanks to the rooftop solar panels that power your home's heating system. After gulping down your breakfast, you head for school. Your classroom is lit using electricity generated by the long line of wind turbines on a nearby hillside. During math class, you add and multiply on your solar-powered calculator. After school, your dad picks you up in his new solar-powered car.

Some of these devices are available now but are used by only a small number of people. Others are still being developed. However, the scenario described here will likely become more and more realistic in the years ahead as renewable energy sources become a part of everyday life.

HIGHLIGHTS IN WIND ENERGY

1100	1888	1930s	1971
Wind power technology reaches Europe, where it is used mainly to grind grain.	American inventor Charles Brush builds the first wind turbine that generates electricity.	Small wind turbines are built by the thousands across the Great Plains to provide farms with electricity.	The world's first offshore wind farm begins operating off the coast of Denmark.

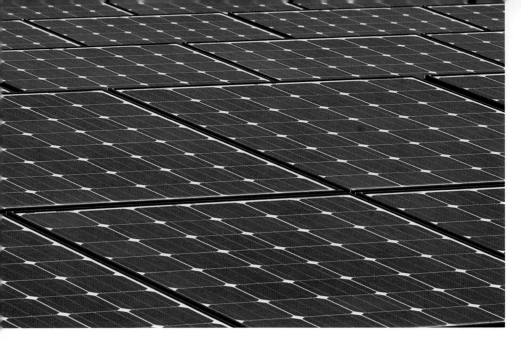

Solar arrays vary widely in size.

SOLAR POWER

Solar energy is the fastest-growing source of renewable energy today. By 2014, more than 500,000 homes and businesses in the United States were powered at least partially by solar energy. On average, a new solar project is installed every 3.2 minutes nationwide, and the use of solar power among the top 25 corporations in America more than doubled between 2012 and 2014.

Solar energy is being used to generate electricity in two ways. The first is through photovoltaic cells that generate electricity directly from sunlight. Solar panels made up of many photovoltaic cells are installed on the roofs of buildings. A number of these panels connected together is called an array. Solar panels and arrays are mainly used to power homes and businesses.

The second method of harnessing solar energy is less direct. It is called concentrating solar power (CSP). In this process, solar energy is used to heat water and form steam that powers turbines to generate electricity. CSP is most often used in larger solar power plants.

HEATING UP

In addition to generating electricity, solar power can be used as a source of heat. Transpired solar collectors are walls made up of flat plates with small holes in them. The plates are heated by sunlight. As air is pushed through the holes, it is heated by the plates. The warm air then travels through vents to provide heat in buildings.

A solar furnace is a device that captures solar energy and uses it to generate temperatures up to 6,300°F (3,500°C). This extremely strong heat can be used to conduct science experiments and produce products such as steel and ceramics. A solar furnace is made up of many mirrors. The mirrors are angled so they reflect solar rays into one another to form a single beam of powerful light. The largest solar furnace in the world today is located in southern France. It has a field of 10,000 mirrors that reflect sunlight toward a curved central mirror.

Solar furnaces can generate extremely high temperatures.

LIGHT IS REFLECTED TOWARD THIS CURVED MIRROR FROM A FIELD OF SMALLER MIRRORS

FROM THIS TO THAT

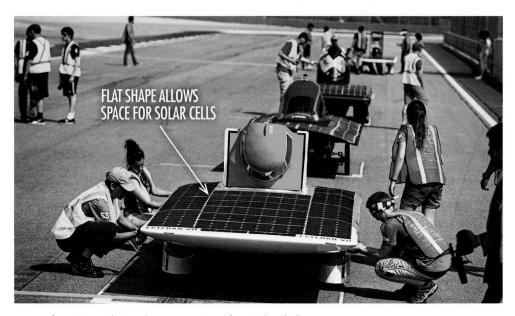

FLAT SHAPE ALLOWS
SPACE FOR SOLAR CELLS

A team from Montreal, Canada, prepares its car for a Solar Challenge race.

SOLAR CARS

Since they were invented in the late 19th century, automobiles have run on many different types of fuel, including gasoline, steam, and electricity. However, a car powered by the sun's energy seemed like a pipe dream until August 31, 1955, when William Cobb of General Motors (GM) unveiled his "Sunmobile" at an auto show in Chicago, Illinois. Just 15 inches (38 centimeters) long, the Sunmobile's roof was equipped with 12 photoelectric cells that created an electric current to power the car's tiny motor. Despite Cobb's small success, decades passed before people began to take solar cars seriously.

THE SOLAR CHALLENGE

Though solar cars didn't exactly take the world by storm after Cobb built the Sunmobile, some scientists and engineers eventually began thinking of ways to make

There is just enough room for a driver in the cockpit of a typical solar-powered race car.

Stella has far more room for passengers than earlier solar cars did.

the technology work in full-size vehicles. Some of these forward-thinking inventors got a chance to show off their experimental creations in 1990 at the first Sunrayce USA, a cross-country race sponsored by GM. This biannual long-distance race (renamed the American Solar Challenge in 2001) is restricted to solar-powered cars. The 2012 race was won by Quantum, a solar car developed by a team at the University of Michigan. It finished the 1,600-mile (2,575 kilometers) course from Rochester, New York, to St. Paul, Minnesota, in less than 45 hours. This record-setting time was 10 hours ahead of the second-place finisher!

STELLA

The cars developed for the American Solar Challenge are all racing cars. They can only hold a single driver. In 2013, Stella, the first solar-powered passenger car, debuted at the World Solar Challenge race in Australia. Developed in part by students at Eindhoven University of Technology in the Netherlands, Stella won the six-day race. The teardrop-shaped car seats four passengers and has an exterior made of lightweight carbon fiber. In 2014, Stella took a trip down the California coast to kick off National Drive Electric Week. It traveled 500 miles (805 km) on a single charge. Clean-running solar cars like Stella may well prove to be the automobiles of the future. ☀

Stella speeds along at a demonstration in Germany.

INTO THE WIND

Wind energy is a fresh breeze blowing across the world of renewable energy. It has a lower environmental impact than solar energy, geothermal energy, or any other renewable energy source. This has helped it become the world's fastest-growing source of clean energy. Forests of wind turbines, called wind farms, are cropping up on the skyline of many U.S. states. They are especially common in California, Texas, Iowa, and Minnesota. However, there is a long road ahead for wind power in the United States. In 2014, wind energy made up only 1 percent of all the energy used in the country.

Wind power is much more common in Europe. Germany has one of the world's largest wind turbines, located near the city of Magdeburg. The diameter of its rotor is 374 feet (114 m), and the turbine stands 407 feet (124 m) above ground level. At this height, wind speeds are greater and more consistent than at lower elevations.

In Denmark, wind turbines provide 28 percent of the total electrical energy used. The nation's leaders hope to raise that figure to 50 percent by 2020.

California is home to many wind farms.

Wind farms are usually located far from towns and cities.

WIND WORRIES

While wind energy is appealing, it is not without problems. Wind does not blow at a constant speed in most regions. It can even stop almost entirely for long periods of time. To assure a constant flow of electricity, some turbines store some of the wind power they absorb so they can provide electricity when there is little or no wind. Others must be used in combination with traditional energy sources to ensure a steady flow of power.

In addition, some people find wind farms an unpleasant sight on the landscape. Others complain about the noise they make. However, scientists are working on designing turbines that create less noise. Also, turbines are usually placed in remote areas where few people live.

Finally, wind turbines are a danger to birds that fly near them or nest in their towers. Engineers are trying to reduce the risk to birds by making wind turbines unsuitable places for nests. Wind energy companies have also started taking the flight paths of birds into account when deciding on locations for new wind farms.

Workers attach sensors to the blades of a turbine.

are connected to a rod called the main drive shaft. As the wind causes the blades to spin, the drive shaft causes a series of gears to begin turning. Each of these gears turns the next one in a series. Because of the size and shape of the gears, each one spins faster than the one before it. The last gear in the series turns a tiny drive shaft that powers the generator. It is this action that finally produces electricity.

TREMENDOUS TURBINES

Today's wind turbines are engineering marvels. They are lightweight, cost-effective, and efficient. There are three main parts to a turbine—the blades, the tower, and the nacelle, which holds the turbine's generator and other mechanical parts. The average turbine rises up to 200 feet (61 m) above the ground and has one to three blades measuring 50 to 80 feet (15 to 24 m) in length. The blades

WIND OVER WATER

Lately, more wind farms are being built along coastal areas and even in open water. These areas are often remote, so they do not affect people's everyday lives. More importantly, they are served by stronger and more consistent winds than inland wind farms. This is because there are fewer obstacles to slow down wind

The world's largest offshore wind farm is located off the coast of the United Kingdom.

over open water. On the downside, the turbines must often contend with powerful waves that could damage them. Their foundations must be reinforced to withstand the water pressure.

One of the biggest water-based wind farms lies in a strait between Denmark and Sweden. Its 20 turbines provide about 4 percent of the annual electrical energy needs of Copenhagen, Denmark's capital city. More recently, companies have started to build floating wind turbines that don't have to be anchored to the seafloor. This allows them to be placed farther away from land. The world's first full-scale floating turbine, Hywind, is located in the North Sea. It supplies electricity to nearby Norway. ✳

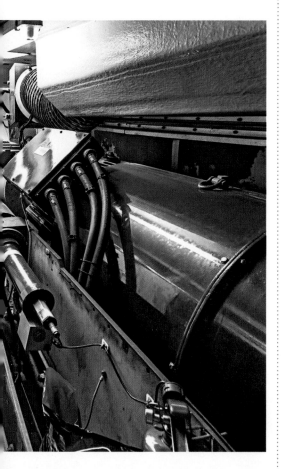

The insides of wind turbines are filled with complex machinery.

DUCTS CARRY SUPERHEATED STEAM
TO TURBINES IN A POWER PLANT

Reykjavik Energy's Hellisheidi power plant is one of the many geothermal plants in Iceland.

GEOTHERMAL POWER

While the sun shines and the wind blows all across the globe, geothermal energy is presently restricted to regions where water makes contact with the hot molten rock under Earth's crust. These underground power sources are called geothermal **reservoirs**. Geothermal power plants must be built on top of such reservoirs. There are geothermal power plants in more than 20 countries, including Israel, Italy, Mexico, Japan, the Philippines, and the United States. In addition, many other nations are developing geothermal plants of their own.

Iceland holds a unique position in the world of geothermal energy. Despite its tiny size, this island nation is one of the world's biggest producers of geothermal energy. This is because it sits atop a volcano, and geysers and hot springs abound. Some 66 percent of Iceland's electricity is produced by geothermal power, and about 85 percent of the country's homes are heated by geothermal energy.

THREE WAYS IT WORKS

There are four types of geothermal power plants. Dry steam plants pipe steam directly into a turbine. After passing through the turbine, the steam is cooled and becomes water again. The water is pumped down into the ground and heated again by hot rocks to make more steam.

Flash power plants work a little differently. Machinery at these plants pumps hot water into special tanks that cause the liquid to turn into steam very quickly. This steam powers a turbine. Some plants use a double flash method. In these situations, any leftover liquid that doesn't turn into steam in the first tank is sent to a second tank, allowing for even more steam to be created.

Binary power plants make use of geothermal reservoirs that are not hot enough for the other two methods. The water in these reservoirs is still very hot, however. It is used to heat a special chemical liquid that then boils into a gas. This gas spins the plant's turbine. The fourth type is a combined flash and binary cycle.

Wairakei Power Station is a flash power plant located in New Zealand.

Workers use special climbing gear to reach the tops of wind turbines when repairs are needed.

TURBINE IS ABOUT
344 FEET (105 M) TALL

WORKER IS ABOUT
197 FEET (60 M)
ABOVE THE GROUND

CHAPTER THREE

ON THE JOB

n 2013, there were an estimated 235,000 people working in the wind, solar, and geothermal energy industries in the United States. In the 21st century, these industries are growing steadily as new power plants are built and existing buildings are **renovated** to accommodate new power sources. As this growth continues, there will be more jobs than ever for people with knowledge of alternative energy. Talented designers and engineers are needed to plan these projects, while skilled workers and machine operators complete construction. Expert technicians install and maintain solar units, while other professionals oversee the operation of completed power plants. In addition, scientists and engineers will continue conducting research and developing new technology to make alternative energy sources even more efficient and inexpensive. With so many potential jobs available, a career path awaits anyone interested in changing the way we use energy.

GEOTHERMAL MILESTONES

1860s	1904	1960	2000
The power from hot springs is first harnessed to heat homes and bathhouses in the United States.	The process for creating a geothermal electric power plant is invented by Italian scientist Piero Ginori Conti.	The first large-scale geothermal power plant in the United States opens for business north of San Francisco, California.	The U.S. Department of Energy launches its GeoPowering the West program to encourage development of geothermal resources in western states.

INVESTIGATING THE POSSIBILITIES

Research is one of the first steps in any project involving science or technology. As a result, alternative energy companies employ scientists in a wide range of specialties to assist with studying new possibilities. These scientists might be hired full time at a power plant or laboratory. They might also work for shorter periods as consultants.

For example, scientists play key roles in deciding where to build a geothermal plant or wind farm. Choosing the right site is especially critical in geothermal power plants. Constructing wells to release geothermal energy from underground is an expensive process. To create an effective plant, these wells must be drilled in the most productive places. **Geologists** study potential sites to see if they are vulnerable to earthquakes, which tend to occur often in areas where there is geothermal activity. **Hydrologists** examine the availability and quality of water in geothermal reservoirs. Environmental scientists and wildlife biologists study the impact that building a geothermal plant or wind farm would have on the area's **ecosystems**. The studies on environmental and animal impact they create are essential in obtaining the necessary government building permits.

Researchers inspect current power plants to help plan improvements.

An engineer inspects turbine blades at a geothermal power plant.

Research is also an important part of designing new materials and technology. For example, stronger, more efficient wind turbines are necessary for the future of the wind energy industry. Atmospheric scientists conduct studies to learn how wind blows differently under various conditions. Such information is used to design turbine components that can withstand wind stress. Material scientists search for new, durable materials that will not wear out and will generate the most energy.

The solar energy industry is constantly searching for ways to improve the design and efficiency of solar cells and the panels they form. Chemists, physicists, and material scientists are among the many people hired to work on these projects.

Art Linares is co-owner of Greenskies, a solar energy company in Connecticut. Greenskies has installed solar energy systems at many businesses, including Walmart and Target stores along the U.S. East Coast.

When did you first realize that you wanted to work in the solar energy industry? In the summer of 2008, when the nation fell into an economic recession and the stock market crashed, I decided to enter the renewable energy field with my brother-in-law. The issue of global warming and the high cost of oil needed to be addressed. As a young **entrepreneur**, I thought I could make a difference. I was attracted to solar energy specifically because it was easy to understand and solar panels involve no moving parts. That meant there would be little need for repairs and few other problems once the solar cells were installed.

What kinds of classes did you take in high school and college that prepared you for a career in the renewable energy industry? When I was a junior in high school, I took a class in life sciences. One day, we watched a film on global warming and the uncertain future of planet Earth. That film had a profound effect on me. I felt I needed to do something to help us prepare for the future and find alternate sources of energy. I wanted to help save the planet and create jobs for people. In college, I was a business major with a focus on entrepreneurship. While still in college I started our solar energy company, Greenskies. It was great because I got to work out my business plan in school and turn it into a reality.

What did you learn in other jobs you held in school that helped you in your career? My father was in the real estate business and bought houses and renovated them to resell. I worked with him and learned about construction and building things. I also worked for a local marina in high school. That got me thinking about one day starting my own business.

What solar energy project have you worked on that you're especially proud of? The Solar Field Project in East Lyme, Connecticut, is the one I'm most proud of. Our company took 43 acres [17 hectares] of undeveloped land and worked with a local utility company to turn it into a solar field with ground-mounted solar panels. It produces 5 **megawatts** of electricity that serves about 18,000 homes in the area. The project has provided jobs for hundreds of people.

It takes a team of people to produce solar energy. Does working as part of a team come naturally to you, and how do you handle the other team members when you're the boss? I first learned how to work with other people on a team in high school athletics—football, basketball, and baseball. I feel at Greenskies we have an effective team whose members work extremely well together. That's why we've been so successful.

What would your dream project be if you were given unlimited resources? I can think of two dream projects. One is to use solar energy to power a plant to process clean water for our country and other less fortunate countries. The problem of water is another major issue I want to get involved with in the future. The other project would be to create electric vehicles that use solar energy. I'd even use solar energy to power the charging stations for electric autos.

What advice would you give to young people who want to work in the field of solar energy? I would tell them to work on the fundamentals of education in school—reading and writing. They will need these skills when they study new technologies and renewable energy. I would encourage them to apply for an internship in a solar company such as ours. We hire young people out of college and even high school students. They should also meet people in the industry and find a mentor who can help them. ✺

Engineers oversee every step of a new wind farm's construction.

ENGINEERS AT WORK

In addition to scientists, alternative energy companies employ a large number of engineers. These experts use math, science, and technical knowledge to design and build everything from the smallest pieces of a solar panel to enormous geothermal power plants. They help oversee the planning and construction of new alternative energy facilities. They also help design better equipment and come up with ways to install it in new places. Like scientists, engineers can be either full-time employees at energy companies or consultants brought on to help complete specialized tasks. For example, an energy company might temporarily bring in environmental engineers to help plan construction methods that do not disturb local wildlife.

FOCUSED ON A SPECIALTY

Like scientists, engineers have different specialties and areas of expertise. As a result, a single project might require input from many different types of engineers. Electrical engineers might plan the way electricity flows from a wind turbine, while mechanical engineers design the way the turbine's moving parts fit together. During the process, these people might consult with material engineers to find the right metals or plastics to build these pieces.

Civil engineers are responsible for the actual construction of power plants, wind farms, and other large energy facilities. They also help develop supporting structures and roadways leading to the facilities. For example, geothermal plants are often built in regions with rocky, difficult terrain. Civil engineers must find a way to build sturdy roads that will afford easy access to these regions. They must also ensure that a plant can withstand possible earthquakes.

Engineering technicians assist engineers in their work. They may be asked to do things such as set up solar equipment or collect weather data for a wind energy project.

Engineers conduct tests on equipment to make sure it is functioning properly.

PUTTING A POWER PLANT IN PLACE

Before a geothermal power plant can be built, workers must drill down into the earth to create the wells that will bring the geothermal energy to the surface. Trained operators handle the specialized construction equipment used to create these wells. They also install special pipes to bring the hot groundwater up to the surface. Workers called roustabouts carry away unwanted by-products such as mud from the work site. They are also responsible for cleaning equipment and work areas.

As the underground work is completed, construction workers clear the land for the power plant site. They then build the plant and the electrical lines used to distribute the electricity it produces. Carpenters, electricians, plumbers, and other workers all play a role in this process. Pipe fitters build the pipes that will carry hot groundwater and steam throughout the plant. Construction managers oversee the work of equipment operators and other laborers.

Once the plant is finished, workers are needed to keep it running. Because of their stable nature, geothermal plants need less upkeep and maintenance than other kinds of power plants. However, workers must still regularly inspect all areas of the plant and monitor its operations.

DRILL CREATES A PATH TO GEOTHERMAL ENERGY UNDERGROUND

Skilled equipment operators play important roles in the creation of new power plants.

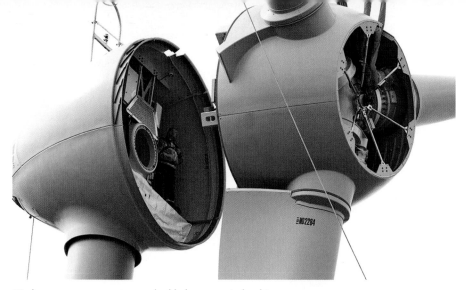

Workers use a crane to mount the blades on a wind turbine.

MANUFACTURING

Wind turbines are brought to wind farms in pieces and assembled on-site. Large turbine companies typically hire smaller companies both in the United States and abroad to produce the parts that make up a complete turbine. Skilled machinists, tool operators, assemblers, and welders carefully follow engineers' designs to produce these parts. This is often a complex process. The nacelle alone is made up of many mechanical components, including gears and generators that must be made separately and then assembled.

Solar panels are also highly complex devices that require many skilled workers to manufacture them. The most important of these workers are called semiconductor processors. These workers first produce the cylinders of silicon, called ingots, that are the main materials in the solar cells. Then they slice the silicon into thin wafers, connect the wafers to metal strips, and place them in the cells. Finally, they join the cells together to form the solar panels. Semiconductor processors also oversee the automated installation of the panels' electrical circuitry and test the completed panels to see that they are working properly.

THE ARTISTIC SIDE

Theo Jansen makes an adjustment to one of his Strandbeests.

A number of visual artists are using renewable energy sources to create art that reflects these powers and reminds people of their importance in ensuring the future of our planet.

SOLAR SCULPTURE

Kathleen and William Laziza are in the forefront of interactive art involving technology. Their *AC/DC Window* is a moving sculpture that is powered using small solar panels. It has been on display in the couple's Micro Museum in Brooklyn, New York, since 1994. "Our interest in solar energy began in the early 1970s," they say, "when we first designed solar

fountains and other kinetic devices. . . . As artists we are interested in new applications and discussions revolving around energy."

BEASTS ON THE BEACH

Since 1990, Dutch artist Theo Jansen has been creating an incredible series of what he calls Strandbeests, which in English means "beach beasts." These huge animal-like sculptures are fashioned from materials such as plastic tubes, cloth sails, and pieces of wood. As their sails catch the wind, they lumber along the beaches where Jansen has set them down. These strange "creatures" have become more advanced over time. Jansen claims that they can sense water and turn away from it as they walk. They can even sense an approaching storm, stop moving, and anchor themselves to the sand. One newspaper has called Jansen's creations "an entirely new line of animals: immense multi-legged walking critters designed to roam the Dutch coastline, feeding on gusts of wind."

ART FOR THE GEOTHERMAL AGE

Photographer Andrea Sirois loves nature. This passion is reflected in her pictures of plants, trees, and green landscapes. In 2014, this Canadian artist turned her talents to creating a mural for the Alexandra District geothermal energy station in British Columbia, Canada. The mural was installed in panels surrounding the building. Its bright colors might look like an abstract pattern at first, but they are actually photographs of moving water. ☀

In 2012, Jansen displayed a 39-foot (12 m) Strandbeest in Melbourne, Australia.

Science, math, and engineering classes provide future scientists and engineers with the knowledge they need to work in the alternative energy industry.

IN THE CLASSROOM

College is an important first step for most people who want to work in the alternative energy industry. Bachelor's degrees are sometimes acceptable for entry-level science positions in such fields as geology, environmental science, and wildlife biology. However, master's degrees are preferred for most science jobs, and doctoral degrees may even be required for many positions. In addition, scientists such as geologists often need a special license or certificate issued by a state licensing board. Engineers need a college degree and possibly even more education depending on their specialty.

Construction workers, plant operators, and other laborers may only need a high school diploma to get started. However, those who wish to serve in management positions may also need an associate's or bachelor's degree in a field such as construction, business management, or engineering.

ON-THE-JOB TRAINING

Many manual laborers and plant operators in renewable energy learn their jobs by doing them. However, they usually need some basic mechanical, technical, and computer skills to get started. Computer skills are also key for scientists, who use them to organize and analyze data.

Electricians, plumbers, carpenters, pipe fitters, and other skilled manual workers attend technical schools and learn their trade in **apprenticeships**. An apprenticeship might last anywhere from three to five years. During this time, apprentices work alongside an experienced professional to learn the skills they will need on the job.

Engineers just out of college or with little experience are often hired as **interns**. They work under the careful supervision of senior engineers. As their skills improve, they are given more challenging and complex assignments. Most engineers are expected to stay up-to-date with new technology by taking continuing education courses throughout their careers. Learning new things is crucial because the field of renewable energy is always changing and growing.

Pipe fitters are among the many workers who learn their trade through apprenticeships.

Every building has different energy needs
and other factors that workers must take
into account when installing solar arrays.

CHAPTER FOUR

OLD BUILDING, NEW POWER SOURCE

A solar energy company has to follow local laws and regulations when it installs solar panels on a home or business. It must also tailor each project to fit the shape, location, and other features of the building. Solar power installation becomes even more complicated when it involves a historic building. Such buildings are protected to ensure that their historical value is not diminished by repairs, updates, or other modifications.

Before a historic building can be fitted with solar energy equipment, the project must be approved by historic commissions or boards. This process is one of the biggest challenges a solar company can face, but it is an important part of increasing the use of renewable energy sources.

RENEWABLE ENERGY ON THE GO

3200 BCE	1981 CE	1983	2014
Ancient Egyptians develop the first wind-powered ships.	The first solar-powered airplane, the Solar Challenger, is flown across the English Channel.	Quiet Achiever, the first full-size solar-powered car, is driven 2,553 miles (4,109 km) across Australia in just 20 days.	The Netherlands predicts that all of its electric trains will be powered by renewable energy sources by 2018.

ANALYZING THE SITUATION

When a solar energy company is preparing to install equipment at a historic site, designers and engineers begin by closely examining the structure. They search for the least noticeable location to install effective panels. Solar panels cannot simply be placed anywhere they fit. They must be positioned in a way that allows them to absorb as much sunlight as possible.

A building's roof is usually the best place for solar panels to be installed. However, this is usually the last choice when it comes to historic buildings. Solar panels on the roof can change the look of the building entirely. In addition, the installation process might result in damage to any delicate parts of the roof. Instead, engineers look to the grounds around the building. They can then design a ground-mounted array that is close to the ground and out of view.

At certain larger sites, such as the San Juan Island National Historical Park in Washington State, solar panels have been installed off the site entirely. In such cases, the solar-generated electricity travels to the site through wires.

Engineers must inspect a site carefully to ensure that they do not overlook important aspects of a project during the planning stages.

It is easier to install solar equipment on rooftops that can't be seen from ground level.

WORKING WITH THE ROOF

If there is no space on the ground, the project's engineers might look at adjoining buildings for suitable installation locations. If they have no choice but to install on the historic building itself, they will plan a way to install the panels so they are not easily visible from the street level. On a flat roof, this might mean positioning the panels away from the roof's edge. On a roof with an incline, it might involve keeping the panels as low and close to the roof itself as possible. The engineers will also try to position the panels on the sides of the roof that face the rear of the building rather than the front or a side street.

In some situations, it may simply be impossible to install solar panels on a building without them being visible. In such cases, the solar energy company may recommend installing solar collectors for hot water to heat the building instead of using photovoltaic cells to provide electricity. These solar collectors require fewer panels and can cover a smaller surface of the building.

WHERE THE MAGIC HAPPENS

Students from the Missouri University of Science and Technology work on their entry for the 2013 Solar Decathlon.

THE U.S. DEPARTMENT OF ENERGY

The Department of Energy is a division of the U.S. government that oversees all forms of energy usage in the country, from traditional fossil fuels to the latest in renewable energy technology. Sponsoring research projects and encouraging the growth of alternative energy sources are among its many responsibilities.

THE OFFICE OF ENERGY EFFICIENCY AND RENEWABLE ENERGY

The Office of Energy Efficiency and Renewable Energy (EERE) is a branch of the DOE. It offers technical assistance to individuals, communities, and states to help them adapt to new energy sources. It also provides funding to alternative energy projects and shares information about jobs, education, and training for people who want to work in the field.

The National Renewable Energy Laboratory's Wind Technology Center is home to special equipment for testing new developments in wind power.

EERE's specialists are on the cutting edge of renewable energy technology. The office recently opened new state-of-the-art wind test facilities in Colorado and South Carolina. Another recent project is the EERE-funded Solar Express program in Chicago, which has reduced the expense of solar permits and sped up permit approval for residents who want to install solar panels on their homes.

NATIONAL RENEWABLE ENERGY LABORATORY

The DOE also funds the National Renewable Energy Laboratory in Colorado. This highly advanced lab is the source of some of the world's most cutting-edge renewable energy research. Hundreds of the country's top energy scientists work at the lab. There, they work to create and test new technology and find ways to introduce it to the public.

CONTESTS AND COMPETITIONS

The DOE and EERE sponsor a number of activities to encourage high school and college students to investigate alternative energy sources. For example, the Solar Decathlon is a biannual competition that challenges student teams from 20 universities and colleges to build homes powered only by solar energy. The homes are judged for efficiency in 10 contests.

In the Race to Zero competition, teams of college students are presented with a specific difficulty that might occur when installing an alternative energy system. They then come up with a plan that could be used to address the problem as effectively as possible.

In the GeoEnergy Is Beautiful contest, college students and high school seniors create eye-catching infographics to get word out about geothermal power. Five winning teams are selected to design a communications and outreach strategy for geothermal energy over an eight-week period. ☀

Scientists at the National Renewable Energy Laboratory work on a project designed to improve solar cells.

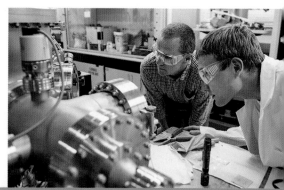

Some people believe that locations such as Joshua Tree National Park would be harmed by the installation of solar panels.

GETTING APPROVAL

Once a plan for installation has been worked out, the solar company must present it to the local historic preservation board or commission for approval before they can begin working. Lawyers or expert consultants go before the board or commission and explain the plan. They detail how much the proposed installation will cost and how much it will save on future energy bills. They also explain how the installation plan will avoid damaging the site's historic value. Finally, they answer any questions the commission has.

If the commission discovers any flaws in the plan, the company must go back to the drawing board to make changes. Then they will make their proposal again at a later date. The process could take months or even years. Some plans are defeated by strong opposition from different groups. For example, one company's plan to bring solar power to Joshua Tree National Park in California was stopped by Native American groups and environmentalists who claimed it would damage historic trails and scenic landscapes.

CODES AND REGULATIONS

Even after the commission approves the proposed plan, the solar company may still have more work to do. Local building codes must be followed carefully. For example, any plumbing or electrical work must meet certain standards. There are also federal regulations for historic sites. The Secretary of the Interior's Standards for Rehabilitation must be met. Rehabilitation is the process of repairing or improving an old building or other property to bring it up to modern standards. The federal standards outline the basic rules for rehabilitating a property while maintaining its original appearance. For example, they require builders to avoid using chemicals or other substances that might damage the building's original color or texture. They also insist that new projects avoid using materials or colors that clash with the site's original appearance.

Workers must be extremely careful when rehabilitating historic buildings that have unique details.

PUTTING IT ALL TOGETHER

Once the plans have been fully approved, the company's installers can finally go to work. Whatever form it takes, the project must be reversible. In other words, future workers must be able to remove it entirely without ruining the existing structure in any way. This allows the possibility of bringing the building up-to-date when even better technology becomes available in the future.

The installers work slowly and carefully. Some historic buildings are rich in small details that could easily be damaged by a tool swung in the wrong direction or a piece of heavy equipment dropped from above. In outdoor settings, the workers must also be careful to avoid damaging the natural landscape, including trees, shrubs, and other plants.

Workers must find ways to get equipment and supplies onto a building's roof without causing any damage.

Solar panels must be kept clean to function properly.

UP AND RUNNING

Once completed, the solar energy system is monitored and regularly inspected by company representatives to make sure it is running properly. If any equipment malfunctions and needs to be replaced or repaired, the project will again be subject to the rules and regulations for historic sites.

Because solar panels have no moving parts, regular maintenance may simply consist of cleaning them several times each year to remove the dirt and debris they often collect. Solar companies sometimes use automated cleaning systems that work like lawn sprinklers. Other times, they may hire a professional solar panel cleaning company to do this chore. Homeowners with solar panels can do the job with a garden hose, though they must be careful not to spray cold water on hot panels, as this can cause them to crack. The best time to clean solar panels is in the early morning or early evening, when the roof is likely to be cool.

Hot Springs National Park receives more than a million visitors each year.

FROM JAPAN TO GERMANY

Natural hot springs are found on every continent. Beppu, Japan, is home to 2,850 hot springs, while the Frying Pan Lake in New Zealand is the largest single hot spring in the world. Elsewhere in the world, the ancient Romans took over huge parts of the world as they built their empire. They constructed baths using water from hot springs in many places. Among the most notable of these are the springs in Aachen, Germany. The Aachen springs contain a large amount of sulfur, which gives them a peculiar smell.

NATURE'S GEOTHERMAL PLANTS

Long before the first geothermal power plants were built, people around the world enjoyed the benefits of geothermal power in natural hot springs. Pools of water heated by the underground magma contain dissolved minerals, many of which have beneficial effects on the human body. As a result, bathing in hot springs can be a very healthy way to relax.

AMERICAN SPRINGS

Hot springs in the United States serve as both popular tourist attractions and rehabilitation centers for people with disabilities. Hot Springs National Park in Arkansas is commonly called The American Spa. (The word spa is Latin for "heated through water.") Its historic Fordyce Bathhouse was a popular spot from 1915 to 1962 and is today a visitors center for the park. Thermopolis, Wyoming, is home to the largest mineral hot spring in the world. It contains 27 different minerals

The name Thermopolis comes from the Greek words for "hot city."

Hot springs are a common part of Japan's natural landscape.

and reaches temperatures of up to 135°F (57°C). The spa at Warm Springs, Georgia, was made famous by President Franklin D. Roosevelt, who found relief for his polio-ridden legs in its soothing waters.

DANGEROUS WATERS

While hot springs are often relaxing and therapeutic, not all of them are safe for bathing. Hot springs located in volcanic areas can often become far too hot for humans. Their waters can reach boiling temperatures, which could scald or even kill people who enter them! ☀

Barack Obama has made alternative energy an important priority during his presidency.

THE WHITE HOUSE GOES SOLAR

Perhaps the most famous historic building to receive a solar energy system is the White House. Serving as the home of U.S. presidents for more than 200 years, it is one of the nation's most notable buildings. In 2010, President Barack Obama promised the country's people that his commitment to renewable energy sources would extend to his own residency. After four years of working out the details, a solar photovoltaic system was finally installed on the White House roof in 2014. The same year, the White House hosted a Solar Summit, calling for expanded use of solar energy in homes, schools, and businesses across the country. President Obama has set an example that hundreds of private and public companies have promised to follow, with a goal of saving more than $26 billion in electricity by 2030.

OTHER PRESIDENTS WHO WENT GREEN

President Obama was not the first U.S. president to bring solar power to the White House. President Jimmy Carter had solar panels installed on the building's roof in 1979. He hoped it might be "a small part of one of the greatest and most exciting adventures ever undertaken by the American people; harnessing the power of the Sun to enrich our lives." However, President Ronald Reagan ordered that the panels be taken down in 1986. Solar power did not return to the White House grounds until 16 years later, when President George W. Bush had a solar system installed on a nearby maintenance shed.

For all the challenges of installing solar panels on buildings and homes—historical or otherwise—the benefits are worth it. As we learn how to make solar power, wind power, geothermal power, and other sources of renewable energy more accessible, efficient, and affordable, they will truly become the energies of the future.

STEVEN STRONG

When President George W. Bush sought to bring solar energy to the White House grounds, he turned to Steven Strong. Strong is one of the nation's top authorities on adapting homes and businesses to solar energy. Since founding his company, Solar Design Associates, in 1974, Strong has been responsible for a number of firsts in the field of solar energy—including the first private home fueled totally by solar energy, the first solar-powered neighborhood, and the first solar-powered Olympic village. In 2014, Strong was given the Professional Leadership Award by the Northeast Sustainable Energy Association, which described him as "a tireless advocate for renewable energy and exemplary buildings."

THE FUTURE

WHAT'S NEXT?

In his Climate Action Plan of 2013, President Obama set a goal of doubling the nation's generation of renewable electricity by 2020. As part of this plan, tax credits and other incentives have greatly increased the number of U.S. businesses and homes making use of solar energy.

Bold new technology will play a huge role in increasing the use of solar, wind, and geothermal energy by making it more efficient and less expensive. Here are some new developments experts are working on that may affect the growth of renewable energy sources in the not-so-distant future.

A scientist at the National Renewable Energy Laboratory shows off perovskite cells.

NEW LIFE FOR SOLAR CELLS

Scientists have discovered a substance that may replace silicon as the main ingredient in photovoltaic cells. It's called perovskite, and it is potentially more efficient at converting sunlight to energy and cheaper than silicon. Also in the works are solar panels capable of both tracking the sunlight's direction as it shifts during the day and adjusting their position.

Faculty and students at Stanford University in California are developing solar cells that don't overheat in the hot sun. Too much heat reduces the cells' ability to generate electricity and shortens their life span. These new cells have cone-shaped structures inside that filter out heat while allowing energy-rich light rays to pass through.

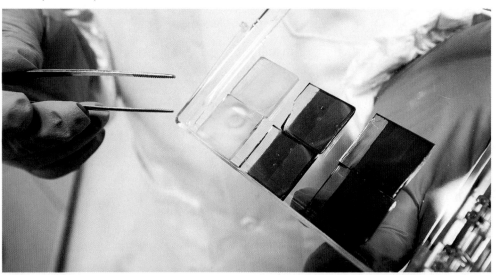

Windstalks could make it easier to bring wind power to towns and cities.

BLADELESS WIND TURBINES

The giant blades of wind turbines are noisy and not always efficient. As a result, energy experts are always searching for ways to capture wind power more effectively. One idea is to use turbines that spin horizontally. Compared to traditional vertical turbines, these new devices work well even when wind speed is low.

Another cutting-edge turbine design is known as the Windstalk. A Windstalk system is made up of tall, thin poles that stick up from the ground. Energy is generated as the poles sway in the wind.

The wind tree is a new wind energy device that is designed to fit easily into crowded urban areas. Shaped like a tree, its "leaves" are actually tiny wind turbines. Unlike traditional wind farms, these devices do not take up much space, and they are very quiet.

GOING DEEPER

Researchers believe that the key to bringing geothermal power to more locations involves drilling down farther beneath Earth's surface. "This is one of the few sources of energy that we really have enough of. The only thing that we need is the technology to harvest it," says Norwegian research scientist Odd-Geir Lademo. Scientists and engineers are working to improve drilling methods in order to make geothermal energy accessible nearly anywhere in the world. ✳

CAREER STATS

SOLAR PHOTOVOLTAIC INSTALLERS

MEDIAN ANNUAL SALARY (2012): $37,900

NUMBER OF JOBS (2012): 4,800

PROJECTED JOB GROWTH (2012–2022): 24%, faster than average

PROJECTED INCREASE IN JOBS (2012–2022): 1,200

REQUIRED EDUCATION: High school diploma or equivalency

LICENSE/CERTIFICATION: None

WIND TURBINE TECHNICIANS

MEDIAN ANNUAL SALARY (2012): $45,970

NUMBER OF JOBS (2012): 3,200

PROJECTED JOB GROWTH (2012–2022): 24%, faster than average

PROJECTED INCREASE IN JOBS (2012–2022): 800

REQUIRED EDUCATION: Some college

LICENSE/CERTIFICATION: None

GEOLOGISTS

MEDIAN ANNUAL SALARY (2012): $94,890

NUMBER OF JOBS (2012): 38,200

PROJECTED JOB GROWTH (2012–2022): 16%, faster than average

PROJECTED INCREASE IN JOBS (2012–2022): 6,000

REQUIRED EDUCATION: Bachelor of science degree

LICENSE/CERTIFICATION: Some states require a license

Figures reported by the United States Bureau of Labor Statistics

RESOURCES

BOOKS

Caduto, Michael J. *Catch the Wind, Harness the Sun*. North Adams, MA: Storey Publishing, 2011.

Doeden, Matt. *Finding Out About Geothermal Energy*. Minneapolis: Lerner Publications, 2015.

Lewis, Rose. *Solar Energy*. Northampton, MA: Pioneer Valley Books, 2011.

FACTS FOR NOW

Visit this Scholastic Web site for more information on wind, solar, and geothermal power:
www.factsfornow.scholastic.com
Enter the keyword **Power**

GLOSSARY

apprenticeships (uh-PREN-tis-ships) arrangements that allow students to study a skill by working alongside an expert

ecosystems (EE-koh-sis-tuhmz) all the living things in a place and their relation to their environment

entrepreneur (ahn-truh-pruh-NUR) someone who starts a business and finds new ways to make money

generators (JEN-uh-ray-turz) machines that produce electricity by turning a magnet inside a coil of wire

geologists (jee-AH-luh-jists) scientists who study Earth's physical structure, especially its layers of soil and rock

hydrologists (hye-DRAH-luh-jists) scientists who study water and its natural movements

interns (IN-turnz) people who are learning a skill or job by working with an expert in that field

megawatts (MEH-guh-wahts) units of electrical power

photovoltaic cells (fo-toh-vol-TAY-ik SELLZ) the smallest components of a solar panel, able to convert sunlight into electricity

renewable (ri-NOO-uh-buhl) coming from sources that can never be used up, such as wind, tides, sunlight, or geothermal heat

renovated (REN-uh-vay-tid) modernized or restored to good condition by cleaning, repairing, or remodeling

reservoirs (REZ-ur-vwahrz) natural or artificial lakes in which water is collected and stored for use

satellite (SAT-uh-lite) spacecraft that are sent into orbit around Earth, the moon, or another body in space

turbines (TUR-buhnz) engines powered by water, steam, wind, or gas passing through the blades of a wheel and making it spin

INDEX

Page numbers in *italics* indicate illustrations.

INDEX (CONTINUED)

ABOUT THE AUTHOR

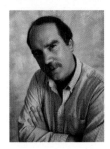

STEVEN OTFINOSKI has written more than 160 books for young readers, including books on blizzards, forensics, computers, and rockets. He lives in Connecticut.